Bits, Tips and Power Points

500 Practical Ideas and Insights for Nonprofit and Association Leaders

Richard J. Maladecki

American Society of Association Executives
1575 Eye Street, N.W.
Washington, DC 20005-1168
202/626-ASAE

ISBN 0-88034-103-3

To my loving family, Logan, Courtney,
and especially my wife, Rosemary.

Contents

Acknowledgments vi

Foreword vii

Ideas and Insights 1

Resources 181

Acknowledgments

To the following friends and family for their continued support:

Mary Malfara
Suzanne Sylvester
David Ree, CAE
Bill Reardon, CAE
Patricia Mogan
The Board of the Electrical
    Association of Philadelphia
Pete Curcio of Junior Achievement

The present and past staff of the
    Electrical Association of
    Philadelphia
Susan J. Ellis of Energize, Inc.
Mark Halsay of Eastern College,
    St. Davids, Pa.
James and Dorothy McGettigan
My parents, Richard and Delphine
    Maladecki

I also wish to thank the faculty and director of the Nonprofit Management Program at Eastern College in St. Davids, Pa., for their encouragement, ideas, and help in assembling and writing this book. They provided me with an excellent opportunity to study and question the practice of nonprofit management, to network with other experienced professionals, and to broaden my perspective.

Foreword

This book is written for the nonprofit professional. Five hundred ideas that will greatly enhance your nonprofit career are presented. These thoughts come from my twenty years of experience as a nonprofit professional. Many of the ideas are staff-related because to be a successful executive, it is critical to maintain a viable, enthusiastic, and committed nonprofit team. We live in an era of information overload. In light of this, this book offers simple suggestions, not theory, that can be used immediately to enhance your career as a nonprofit executive.

Richard J. Maladecki

Mount a plaque of your organization's
mission statement in the lobby
or reception area.

■

Ask key nonboard-member volunteers
to serve as ad hoc members to
board committees.

■

Make sure your organization's logo
appears in the background in
organization photographs.

Purchase, or obtain as a donation, a podium for your organization's training room.

■

Subscribe to the *Chronicle of Philanthropy* and the *Nonprofit Times*.

■

At golf outings, conduct a 50/50-type raffle where your organization keeps half of the proceeds.

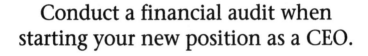

Conduct a financial audit when
starting your new position as a CEO.

Always look people in the eye
when speaking to them.

■

Give staff and volunteers polo-style shirts
featuring your organization's name or logo.

■

Send out one sincere thank you note a day.

■

Attend at least one nonprofit-related
seminar every six months.

Designate staff meetings as "team meetings."

■

Always be involved in your
budget-making process.

■

Two months before a special event,
place a prominent reminder of the event
on your fax cover page.

■

Install tack strips in your meeting
rooms so that it's easy to post charts
and other helpful visuals.

Secure the services of a loaned executive
from a corporate "big brother."
You should establish precise, measurable
objectives for this loaned executive.

Maintain a detailed volunteer job descriptions file for each type of volunteer position. Include duties, number of hours needed a month, and location.

◼

Use a professional photographer to cover important organization events. Establish in advance what photographs are needed.

◼

Research and understand your organization's direct (or indirect) competition.

Occasionally purchase tickets to professional sporting events or cultural events for your volunteers.

■

Keep monthly financial reports simple; make them user-friendly.

■

Always return phone calls within twenty-four hours.

Enlist a volunteer or hire an employee
to serve as your organization's
director of volunteers.

■

Send personal holiday and birthday cards
to your primary stakeholders.

■

Lease a voice mail service. Record a
message that promotes your organization's
activities when calls are put on hold.

Drive a four-door car.

■

Send out the board meeting agenda
two weeks before the meeting.

■

Include a pocket on the inside back cover of
your annual report or membership directory
so that members have a convenient place
to store notes and other information.

■

Distribute your newsletter on a set schedule.

Volunteer with at least one other nonprofit organization. (This will give you an additional nonprofit perspective.)

Establish a monthly private meeting
with your board chairperson or president.
Budget one hour to provide pertinent
updates and to seek counsel on issues.

■

Maintain a library of annual reports of
your major stakeholder companies.

■

Maintain a working Strategic Planning
Committee of the board. Review the
strategic plan annually.

Maintain records of time donated by your organization's volunteers.

■

Appoint an individual or become the individual responsible for recording your organization's local history.

■

Display a past presidents plaque in your lobby or reception area.

Send out thank-you-for-your-support
letters within forty-eight hours
(personalize the note, if possible).

■

Include a wish list of items desired by
your organization as potential gifts-in-kind
in its annual report or newsletter.

■

Encourage the board's vice-president
to become a member of the
Strategic Planning Committee.

Develop viable communication channels
that allow volunteers to voice ideas,
suggestions, and concerns—
perhaps a written monthly report.

■

Require all organization checks to carry
two signatures: one board member's
and one staff member's (officers and
executive staff should be eligible).

■

Place a customized logo mat in your lobby.

As a daily personal reminder, place the
following statement in a prominent place:

"A Good Board Is Not A Gift
But A Victory"

Strongly encourage 100 percent board
donor participation in a fund drive.

■

Conduct a thorough board orientation
for new board members.

■

Maintain accurate staff attendance records.

■

Ask each board member to "sit"
on at least one standing committee.

Organize a program or activity
evaluation committee.

■

Issue an annual board member report card.
Subjects should include attendance,
donations, corporate support, etc.

■

Meet with your predecessor.

■

Hold at least one formal volunteer
appreciation function annually.

Learn and use the names of the spouses
of your primary volunteers.

■

Review your mission statement.

■

Always carry your business card.

■

Encourage staff to further their education,
especially in the nonprofit management field.

Remember that gifts-in-kind are as
valuable as cash contributions.

■

Be fax-sensitive in selecting
your color paper purchases.

■

Maintain accurate monthly financial reports
and distribute them on a timely basis.

Consider the legal ramifications when
official activities involve serving alcohol.

■

Consider sponsors (corporate friends)
when planning each activity
or segments of an activity.

■

Periodically, invite nonboard member
volunteers to board meetings to
recognize their contributions.

At golf outings, implement a 50/50
putting contest, on the practice green,
to raise additional revenue.

■

Have a nonstakeholder moderate the
strategic planning process.

■

Become involved in local or national
nonprofit professional organizations.

Print a professional board book,
featuring tabbed sections on board members,
committee assignments, committees,
board minutes, committee minutes,
and your newsletter.

Include artwork or graphics on
each page of your newsletter.

■

Understand the difference between
tax-exempt and nontax-exempt
nonprofit organizations.

■

Should a major stakeholder die,
personally attend the funeral.

Develop, publish, and maintain
an annual schedule of activities
before the start of the program year.

■

Print your mission statement in each
newsletter and each annual report.

■

Promote activities with before-and-after
coverage of events in local newspapers.

Display photos of your current board
officers in your lobby.

■

Consult the Mandel Center for Nonprofit
Organizations for information relevant
to nonprofit organizations.

■

Purchase a directors' and officers' liability
insurance policy for board members.

■

Obtain stationery printing as a gift-in-kind.

Develop and maintain formal
name badges for board members,
key staff, and special volunteers.

■

At a meeting, present a slide show
featuring the year's activities.

■

Reduce expenditures by asking board
members to host meetings and
related board activities.

Write job descriptions for each staff position.

■

Develop and maintain working
board committees.

■

Become active in your Chamber
of Commerce. Doing so may provide
you with valuable contacts.

■

Consider an official credit card program,
featuring royalties for your organization.

Secure continuing education units
for your educational programs.

■

Address all issues identified in the
annual audits management letter.

■

Never offer the board options
without thoroughly justifying
one recommended option.

Insist that each member of the support staff knows the who, what, where, when, and how of each activity, thus enabling all staff to answer inquiries.

Initiate a periodic casual dress day for staff.

■

Reduce expenses by switching
to once-a-month payroll.

■

Incorporate an in-house training
facility with a kitchen.

■

Build strong relationships with secretaries
of board members. Each should
become your ally and liaison.

Include birthday greetings to
stakeholders in your newsletter.

■

Evaluate the need for an
employer/employee contract.

■

Use the calendar year as the fiscal year.

■

Conduct an annual, first-class staff retreat,
to plan the upcoming operations year.
Ask a corporate friend to donate the facility.

Order customized fortune cookies featuring
your organization's message and distribute
them as a dessert at an organization event.

■

Volunteer to be a presenter
for a nonprofit seminar.

■

Compose timely and interesting
articles for a nonprofit publication.

■

Reread this book twice a year.

Join the American Society of
Association Executives.

■

Consider adding to the front page
of your newsletter: Route to: _____

■

Annually compose or refine job
descriptions for committee chairpersons.

■

Develop a Diversity Task Force.

Conduct an annual holiday or
appreciation party or an open house
for volunteers and staff.

■

Strongly encourage guest articles to be
printed in your organization's newsletter.

■

Add you organization's mission
statement to its stationery.

Develop working relationships
with other nonprofit organizations.

■

Review annual income in relation to funding
sources; if one funding source comprises
more than a third of total income,
develop long-range plans to
decrease that percentage.

■

Consider an image consultant for yourself.

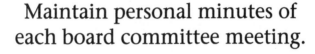

Maintain personal minutes of
each board committee meeting.

Sell advertising space in your
organization's newsletter.

■

For recurring events, preprint outside
brochure covers, then customize
the brochure by printing current
information inside the shell.

■

Keep an extra tie or pair of stockings
in your desk for emergencies.

Give key stakeholders wall plaques
that recognize their contributions.

■

Use a message board in the lobby to
welcome stakeholders to your offices.

■

Remember that the nonprofit's federal
tax return form is due before the
15th day of the 5th month.

Get to know your state representative
and senator. Encourage each to serve on the
Advisory Council, or invite each to key annual
affairs. At the very least, place each on your
organization's newsletter mailing list.

Display an American flag on a floor stand
in your lobby or training center.

■

Develop a thorough understanding
of your organization's by-laws.

■

When hiring for professional positions,
remember to hire the person who meets both
the short-term needs (1-12 months) and the
long-term needs (1-5 years). Do not compromise
your long-term needs to satisfy the short-term.

Send out at least one press release,
with photo, per month.

■

Develop a partnership with a local college
or university to secure student interns.

■

Update your organization's master press
release mailing list annually. Confirm names,
addresses, and phone and fax numbers.

Always include on every communication
your organization's name, address, city, state,
zip code, and phone and fax numbers.

■

Print small stickers featuring the who,
what, where, and when of an event
for stakeholders' personal calendars.

■

Draft and approve a fiduciary
responsibility statement.

Start and end all meetings on time.

■

Compose and approve a conflict-of-interest
statement for volunteers, board, and staff.

■

Develop and maintain an effective
invoice system of 30, 60, and 90 days,
followed by phone contact.

Promote the nonprofit industry
as often as you can.

Remember that foundations expect
a diverse board and a financially
well-operated organization.

■

Present a quality gift or plaque to your
board president or chairperson at the
end of his or her term in office.

■

For an organization-sponsored event
lasting more than one day (trade shows,
conventions, etc.), lease pagers for key staff.

Develop and maintain a
board meeting format.

■

Secure professional talent to manage
long-term investments.

■

Secure golf outing dates at least
one year before the event.

■

Always remember that you're
in the people business.

Treat your co-workers to donuts
or muffins once a week.

■

Set and maintain a regular schedule
for team meetings.

■

Review each segment of board and
board-related meeting agendas with
each chair before the meeting.

Partner with a major newspaper to produce an annual feature supplement.

■

Use customized license plate frames to promote your organization.

■

Request and expect discounts on all purchases for your organization.

■

Sell hole-sponsor signs at golf outings for additional revenue.

———■———

Meet annually with each board member.
To receive his or her full attention,
meet for breakfast or lunch at a neutral site.

———■———

Evaluate your board list on an annual basis—ask the question: Are all needed players on board?

◼

If your organization is a chapter of a national agency, meet periodically with executives from neighboring chapters. Exchange information, develop mutually beneficial partnerships (marketing, public relations, etc.), and share concerns.

Contract with a local winery
to supply bottles of wine with
customized labels for special events.

■

Offer volunteers a quarterly lecture
series, featuring interesting and timely topics
and speakers from your organization or
from your organization's affiliates.

■

Secure from the Mayor's Office or the
Governor's Office a proclamation declaring
your organization's day or week.

Coordinate your organization's
appearance on a local news magazine
television program once a year. Invite your
volunteer leadership to participate.

■

Join the National Society of
Fund-Raising Executives.

■

Use outdated envelopes (those with
old addresses, old designs, etc.)
for payroll purposes.

Maintain a separate nonprofit references drawer—label the folders: management, fund development, communications, volunteerism, board development, training attended, wish list, and miscellaneous.

◼

Make arrangements with a local food or convenience store chain to print material promoting your organization on their grocery bags.

Demonstrate support for your city or region by displaying artwork featuring scenes of the area. Become a regional booster.

■

As a special fundraising event, coordinate and implement a secretaries' luncheon during National Secretaries' Week. Consider a fashion show, hosted by a local department store, to serve as the entertainment.

■

Maintain an interest-bearing checking account.

Conduct a personal and thorough
cost-benefit analysis for all major decisions.

◼

Communicate regularly and sincerely
with donors with birthday cards,
holiday cards, and newsletters.

◼

Conduct an annual independent
financial audit or review.

Design a customized thank you note
with matching envelope,
featuring your business card.

■

When evaluating a new fundraising activity,
consider hiring a contract employee to
initiate and manage the activity. If the activity
proves successful, consider employing the
individual on a permanent basis.

■

Each week, implement one idea
from this book.

Consider enrolling in a Dale Carnegie
Human Relations Course
(scholarship opportunities may be available).

■

Ask each staff member to contribute
to your organization's annual fund
development campaign. Strive for
100 percent staff participation.

■

Develop and market to the
general public holiday cards
as a fund-development concept.

Develop a volunteer speakers corps.
Properly screen and train each individual.
Then, promote. Develop a goal of one
speaking assignment per month.

Give staff customized watches
featuring your organization's logo.

■

Offer a monthly or quarterly donation
payment schedule when accepting
pledges from individuals.

■

Subscribe to the Nonprofit Survival Network.

■

Familiarize yourself with the
National Center for Non-Profit Boards.

Ask a local personality to serve as your organization's official spokesperson. This person may sit on the board, promote an annual activity (social event, golf outing, trade show), or serve as a media representative.

■

Publicly thank members of the board and staff for work-related contributions, especially at the conclusion of a special event.

Purchase and distribute logo lapel pins.

■

Consider rotating board committee
assignments every two years.

■

During the board nomination process,
clearly communicate time and funding
expectations to each candidate.

■

Invite and encourage volunteers to make
financial donations to your organization.

Regularly use cable public-access channels and/or cable community bulletin boards to promote your organization's activities.

■

Thoroughly understand that 501(c)(3) organizations must "not participate in or intervene in any political campaign on behalf of or in opposition to any candidate for public office."

■

Twice a year, after board meetings, evaluate how the meeting turned out.

Involve board members in decision-making
processes as soon as possible.

■

Use a bank lock box service to receive
incoming cash and check donations
to your organization.

■

For added community visibility, print
and distribute membership certificates or
plaques to participating individuals.

Maintain a personnel policy manual.
Review it annually with members
of the Executive Committee.

■

Add a twelve-month calendar (one page,
perforated) to your annual report
or yearbook for easy reference. If perforated,
include your organization's address,
phone and fax numbers, and logo.

■

Recognize retiring board members.

Develop your organization's "look."
Use a "signature" graphic and font to make
all correspondence easily recognizable.

Consider an official Board of Directors attendance policy.

■

Implement a cash award system
for cost-saving suggestions from staff.

■

Initiate an employee wellness program.
Ask employees to coordinate
via a Staff Wellness Committee.

Build board team spirit
with programmed social time.

■

In respect to the annual development
campaign, initiate friendly competition
among members of the board
(team assignments).

■

To develop ownership at
board meetings, invite chairpersons
to present committee reports.

Invite your direct subordinates to a breakfast or lunch when conducting annual or semi-annual evaluations.

■

On each agenda, list as an agenda item: Next Meeting Date.

■

Keep a city, county, or regional map in your briefcase.

Use a microcassette recorder, especially
for drive-time use. Record your thoughts
and ideas, then establish a pattern of
playing the tape back each morning.

■

Establish your reputation as an
"on time" professional.
Always be punctual for meetings.

■

Maintain accurate personnel files and take the
time to update them weekly or monthly.

Develop an organized satellite or committee structure, if your organization's geographical size warrants additional support in outlying areas. Extend to the satellite chair or president an invitation to serve as a board member.

■

Secure at a nonprofit rate, or as a gift-in-kind, advertising at the regional airport and train station, in the form of billboards.

■

Remember that college students are good volunteer resources.

Stamp outgoing envelopes and
correspondence with a customized
rubber stamp that promotes
a special upcoming activity.

■

Encourage quiet board members to
become involved. Assign these individuals
to co-chair committees.

■

Order and distribute logo ties.

Solicit volunteer and financial support
from local service clubs, such as
Kiwanis, Lions, and Rotary.

Organize a corporate advisory council of senior-level business and professional executives. This nonpolicy-making group should assist in one or two specific areas of the operation, such as a special fundraising event.

■

Establish a strong relationship with one caterer for your organization's food service needs.

■

Contact a movie theater for discount tickets for volunteers and staff.

Make sure your organization's computer software is backed-up weekly.

■

For your own vehicle, order customized license plates featuring your organization's name (abbreviated, acronym, etc.).

■

Read one book about nonprofit management annually.

Ask volunteers to recommend potential volunteers. Formalize the process by developing a referral form.

■

Print posters to promote an organization activity. Then, post these in store windows (enlist the help of volunteers to place the posters).

■

Have on hand and refer to
The Foundation Directory.

Develop a "friends of" the organization group. This group could assist with an annual fundraising special event.

■

Conduct yearly a brief board orientation or reintroduction to understanding your organization's financial statements.

■

Pay travel expenses for key volunteers.

■

Consider a for-profit subsidiary.

Order customized "business card"
coffee mugs for volunteers and staff.

■

Consider a code of ethics
for your board, staff, and stakeholders.

■

Host nonprofit group gatherings
at your facility.

■

Participate in a Leadership, Inc., class.

Have your organization participate
in an "adopt a highway" program.

∎

Continuously evaluate programs, special
events, and fundraisers. Routinely conduct
post-event committee meetings.
Make it a part of the planning process.

∎

Use table tents for preassigned seating
at board meetings.

Start an employee-of-the-month campaign.
Offer guidelines and a quality award.

Develop master "to do" lists for use
before board meetings, volunteer recognition
events, special events, trade shows, etc.
Refine each yearly.

Consider the benefits of a remote radio
broadcast at one of your
organization's major functions.

Compose a customer service
philosophy statement; post it in the
lobby and print it in the newsletter.

Conduct an officers' orientation, after new officers are elected. Develop goals and objectives for the upcoming terms in office.

■

Evaluate each standing board committee and task force annually to determine if the issues on which they focus are still relevant.

■

Budget a set surplus for each program activity.

Include foundation representatives in the early stages of your grant-writing process.

◼

Strive for positive and effective community relationships.

◼

Verify that twenty-four-hour emergency phone numbers have been forwarded to the building management, local police, insurance representative, etc.

Keep board members informed
of significant news between
formal meetings of the board.

■

Maintain a talent pool of qualified,
part-time, on-call workers.

■

Yearly, coordinate a group board photograph.
This should be done immediately after a
board meeting, with prior written notice.

Periodically, host a staff and spouse gathering
(holiday dinner or barbecue) at your home.

■

On the election of new officers or members
of the board, coordinate a press release
with a black-and-white photograph
highlighting the election of each individual.

■

Investigate all available matching-gift
opportunities. Market the specific
details to your donor base.

On a regular basis, invite a member who
has successfully completed one of your
organization's educational programs to offer
a testimonial at board meetings (this helps
to create ownership of the program).

■

Frame a copy of the Declaration of
Independence, and hang it in the lobby.

■

Subscribe to *CEO Update.*

Encourage a viable student member
category for post-high school students.

■

Mail minutes of a meeting within
one week of the meeting.

■

Maintain an active board
Nominating Committee.

Keep a plastic-covered name tag
in your briefcase.

When traveling (professional or personal),
give staff both a phone number and
fax number where you can be reached.

■

Invite and encourage board members
to directly participate in one of your
organization's activities.

■

When celebrating your birthday,
invite people to donate to your
organization in lieu of gifts.

Print a map detailing your organization's location on the back of your business card.

Prepare for a staff retreat by establishing an agenda one month before, giving out staff assignments, and securing budgets and last year's calendars.

◼

Maintain a signature bank of key stakeholders on 3-inch by 5-inch cards.

◼

Annually, offer an organized and clearly defined membership campaign.
Ideas to consider: dues discounts, golf outing prizes, sports or theater tickets.

For something different at an organization activity, place a "throw away" camera at each table. Encourage those seated at each table to take photos and then collect the cameras at the end of the event.

■

Organize a weekly staff exercise class.

■

Yearly, calculate a cost per member or a cost per program.

Print customized "post it" type note pads,
promoting your organization
(logo, name, phone, fax, etc.).

■

Prepare the annual budget in a
three-tiered approach: most likely,
least desirable, and utopia.

■

Offer at least one floating holiday
a year to staff.

During photo opportunities, remove name tags
from individuals being photographed.

■

Conduct a professional partnership audit—
should you refine your relationship
with similar types of organizations
for mutual rewards and benefits?
Review this audit annually.

■

Keep an adjustable, pen-size pointer
in your briefcase for presentations.

Purely for fun, organize a putting contest at your organization's trade show or convention.

■

Feature a staff column in your newsletter.

■

Maintain a viable Total Quality Management Task Force (staff, board, and volunteers).

■

Maintain an updated photobank of your organization's key stakeholders.

Always stand to give board presentations.

■

If possible, place long-distance calls
before 8 a.m. and after 5 p.m.

■

Form a Past Presidents Advisory Committee.

■

For major events, buy or rent a
business-card-size luggage tag maker.

Periodically invite staff members
to board meetings.

Display a portrait of your organization's
founder in the lobby.

◼

Process checks twice,
and only twice, a month.

◼

Begin each team meeting by having staff
members give brief descriptions
of recent achievements.

◼

Maintain confidentiality on all staff salaries.

Occasionally, take work-related photographs of your co-workers. Establish a bulletin board area to display these photographs.

■

Secure a radio and television sponsor for your organization's major activities, especially fundraising events.

■

Send a copy of all board committee mailings to the board president.

Keep your pocket calendar up to date
with the phone numbers and addresses
of your key stakeholders.

■

On the Wednesday before Thanksgiving,
give each staff member, and/or
key stakeholders, a frozen turkey.

■

Update and periodically distribute
public service announcements to
local radio and television stations.

Conduct an annual public relations luncheon for members of the media. At the meeting, distribute press kits.

◼

Invite your organization's executive secretary to all board meetings to record minutes.

◼

Conduct a monthly staff brainstorming session; address one process or procedure per session, with the understanding that conclusions generated will be implemented.

As a staff morale builder, hold an annual office "fix up"—enliven the office by painting, rearranging furniture, cleaning files, etc.

■

To reduce postage expenses, group mailings to volunteers and members.

■

Develop and adhere to an affirmative action policy and initiatives.

Always be member-sensitive.

■

Honor past presidents with an annual
luncheon. At the luncheon,
present an organization update
or seek advice on an issue.

■

Remember the "roots" of your organization;
attend and participate in meetings involving
members other than primary stakeholders.

———■———

Annually, ask each staff member
to answer the following question:

"If you could refine one aspect
of your position, what would it be?"

———■———

Hang posters that display your organization's name and logo at meetings and other events.

■

To test the timeliness of mailings (especially bulk or third-class mailings), include the home address of two staff members in each mailing.

■

Mail employment rejection letters in a timely manner.

Videotape major organization activities.
Edit to create promotional tools
for the following year.

■

Conduct a thorough marketing audit
of your organization, including its environ-
ment, objectives, strategies, and activities.
Determine both concerns and opportunities.

■

Develop a tested system to thoroughly
screen potential volunteers.

Make sure each board member
thoroughly understands your
organization's mission statement.

■

During golf outings, hire a photographer
to take photos of each foursome
at the first tee. To raise funds,
sell these photos for a nominal fee.

■

Secure name plates at each staff
member's office or work station.

As part of the job or volunteer interview process, contact each candidate's references. Develop and ask a series of questions regarding needed talents and skills.

■

Add to the openness of a meeting by encouraging participants to fill in their names on blank table tents provided by your organization.

When conducting an official function,
never miss the opportunity to promote
other organization activities.

To maximize your organization's exposure at organization functions, encourage staff members to sit with volunteers (discourage staff tables).

■

When professional consulting assistance is needed, consider retired business executives to do the job. One resource for this is the Executive Service Corporation.

■

Initiate a member psychographics survey to collect needed member and volunteer data.

Coordinate an annual golf outing
specifically for board members in
conjunction with a board meeting or retreat.

■

Annually distribute biographies and resumes
of key staff to your board members.

■

As a courtesy to board members,
mail board-related information on
three-hole-punched paper, so that the pages
can be easily placed in their board manual.

Bring a copy of your organization's
board manual to board-related functions.
(It serves as an excellent resource
and sets an example.)

■

Coordinate a volunteer-of-the-year program
(set specific guidelines).

■

Maintain, in a secured location,
a facility master key inventory.

Periodically, assist support staff
in a mundane task, e.g., folding, stuffing,
and adding postage to a mailing.

■

Feature a calendar-of-events section
in your organization's newsletter.

■

Encourage the use of an
employee/volunteer suggestion box.
Put this box in a prominent spot.

Strive for viable, on-going
organization partnerships.

■

To better evaluate their computer skills and
administrative talents, invite final candidates
for support staff positions to work one or two
days as a temporary hourly employee.

■

During the holiday season,
give each primary stakeholder a poinsettia.

Plan board and volunteer functions
on nonholiday weeks (individuals may
be traveling that week).

■

File the appropriate tax form (Form 1099)
for each contract employee.

■

For fundraising events, print the actual
amount of the donation on tickets
(contact your nonprofit financial expert
for specific and current information).

Evaluate the need for an 800 phone service.

■

On the front page of your organization's
newsletter, feature a "What's Inside"
section that briefly highlights the contents
with appropriate page numbers.

■

To ensure proper follow through while
a staff person is on vacation, request that
he or she leave a day-by-day checklist.

Keep a calculator in your briefcase.

■

Use a rubber stamp with "Board-Related
Information" on the envelopes of all
applicable board correspondence.

■

If your organization is a 501(c)(3) that
files a 990EZ Form, remember that an
accompanying schedule A also must be filed.

———■———

Recognize the efforts of your board members'
secretaries during the holiday season.

———■———

To keep the board informed, compose and
mail a brief (one page) monthly update.

■

Fly a customized corporate flag
at your organization's office.

■

Dust off the current strategic plan and
review its contents. Measure achievements
to the stated goals or objectives.
Determine the viability of the plan
and consider appropriate action.

Place courtesy phone calls to all members
of the board at least twice a year. Discuss
board-related items, needs, ideas, etc.

■

Maintain personal accurate records
of conversations for future use.

■

Consider an annual team bonus plan
for exceptional performance above and
beyond the stated organization objectives.

Before each board meeting, scrutinize
the agenda, anticipate related questions
or issues, and develop appropriate answers
(a good nonprofit manager should not
be surprised during a board meeting).

■

At board meetings, approve your
organization's monthly financial statements.

■

Consider giving the board president
a gavel at each meeting.

As an attention grabber to potential
customers, mail a small bag of peanuts
stapled to a preprinted message that
begins with, "You're nuts if you..."

■

Alternate board meeting sites.

■

Show your employees sincere appreciation
for a job well done, true participation
in the decision-making process,
and an understanding of their supervisor.

Give out a personalized 12-inch cookie
for employee/volunteer recognition
or special dates.

■

Administer the Myers-Briggs test
to your employees (secure results
as a management reference).

■

Enlist a college intern to research
potential new markets.

Respect and maintain employee privacy.

■

Distribute decals with your organization's
logo to your members and volunteers.

■

Commit your organization to at least one
new board member orientation per year.
Items to be covered: fiduciary responsibility,
financial statement walk through, committee
structure, mission statement, introductions.

Remember to "work smarter, not harder."

Use visual aids during each presentation.

At the end of any presentation,
allow adequate time for a question-and-
answer session; these sessions usually are
as meaningful as the presentation itself.

Fully understand IRS Form 990T
(in regard to unrelated business income).

Do not serve alcohol during official
meetings and functions.

■

Use a limousine service for the honoree
or other dignitaries of a major
recognition event.

■

To secure additional revenue at a fundraising
event, consider a "basket of cheer" raffle.
(Fill baskets to be raffled off with gourmet
treats, fruit, and wine.)

To build team morale or to reward staff efforts, give staff gifts that are inspirational or motivational, such as desk plaques or calendars with encouraging messages.

■

Use a laptop computer.

■

Periodically review your long-distance telephone service to ensure your organization is using the most efficient company.

Consider term limits for board members.

■

Understand the differences of trading and
nontrading nonprofit organizations.

■

Use a day planner calendar system.

■

Maintain one file drawer for annual audits,
Form 990s, board or executive minutes,
and monthly financial statements.

Conduct an annual review of your
job description with your manager.

■

Consider housing your organization on or near
a university campus to take full advantage
of the university's various resources.

■

Explore the advantages of
cause-related marketing—
examine the win-win possibilities.

At various organization activities,
make the price of admission a canned
or other nonperishable food item.
Then, donate the goods to a charity.

■

As a team builder during the month
of March, coordinate an office pool
for the NCAA basketball tournament.

■

When vacancies occur, consider candidates
from your organization's volunteer force first.

Purchase or secure as a donation,
a voice-mail system.

Thoroughly investigate and understand
the law relating to nonprofit postage rates
and take full advantage of this benefit.

■

For attention and probable higher return
when conducting a survey, fax one question
per day, for several days, to secure needed
information (call the program
"The Question of the Day").

Regularly conduct an exit-type
interview roundtable session with
members or volunteers who have
chosen not to participate anymore.

■

When recruiting for the board, be prepared to
offer a potential candidate other volunteer
roles if a board position is not appropriate.

■

Feature brief, updated information
about upcoming events in your organization's
recorded telephone message.

Conduct informational interviews to screen
members as potential board members.

■

Develop a volunteer application form
(include name, immediate manager,
birth date, experience, education, etc.).

■

Find out what key volunteers' favorite
junk food or snack is. Then, surprise them by
serving the snack at an appropriate time.

To enhance volunteer recognition,
write each volunteer's manager or personnel
director a note of appreciation.

■

For bookkeeping assistance, contact your local
community accountants organization.

■

Purchase insurance for your trade shows.

■

Familiarize yourself with area law firms
that specialize in nonprofit law.

Hold a ribbon-cutting ceremony to kick off major activities (conventions, trade shows, dedications, etc.).

■

Prepare yourself for conversation and small talk before each board-related meeting; read the newspaper to be knowledgeable of current events.

Consider program alumni to be
potential board members.

■

When initiating a new internal policy
or procedure, introduce the concept as a
pilot program so that staff feel comfortable
with the change. After the trial period
(30, 60, or 90 days), conduct an evaluation
meeting to examine the policy or procedure.

■

Add automatic electronic transfer of funds
as a donation-giving option.

Periodically review your organization's systems and procedures to avoid unnecessary duplication or overlap.

■

Before the start of a sport season, secure or print professional/college sport team schedules, then mail them out as a courtesy to your volunteers/members. (If possible, print your organization's logo on the schedule.)

Continuously refine your grant writing
skills by attending one grant writing
seminar each year.

■

To gain greater confidence in
your public speaking ability,
join the local Toastmasters Chapter.

■

To expedite volunteer or membership
communications, use a fax software package.

Strive to increase the contribution of
each current donor. (Attempt to increase
at a rate of 5 percent a year.)

■

Become familiar with the nonprofit curriculum
offered for bachelor's and master's degrees
by approximately thirty U.S. universities.

■

Insist that all written communications
are proofed twice by different
people before distribution.

Always keep quarters and dimes
in your car for parking meters.

■

Annually review the adequacy of your
organization's insurance coverage.

■

To develop a uniform schedule for events,
conduct the event on the same day each
month or on the same day each year.

■

Allow staff members to take their
own birthday as an extra day off.

———■———

To further your relationship with your board
chairperson, encourage programmed social
time (golf, tennis, dinner, training, etc.).

———■———

For each potential new project, develop a formal review process that tests the idea against the goals and objectives of the strategic plan.

■

Consider an energy audit of your organization's offices to reduce operating expenses. Contact an energy management company, then conduct a cost-benefit analysis.

Recognize your outgoing board president
by inviting his or her supervisor
and/or significant other to his
or her last board meeting.

■

Consider unique meeting sites to enhance
meeting attendance (e.g., golf clubs, new
restaurants, amusement parks, private clubs).

■

Start your organization's Hall of Fame for
outstanding long-term volunteers/members.

Avoid leadership vacuums by
continuously grooming board members
with additional responsibilities.

■

Affiliate your organization with a local
university's business school to offer
a nontraditional educational program.

■

Become familiar with the U.S. Chamber
of Commerce's Institute for Organization
Management education program.

Join your regional or state organization
of association executives.

■

Properly groom leadership: invite your
board vice-president to appropriate meetings,
especially as his or her term end nears.

■

Offer a flexible benefit plan to staff.

■

Assign members of the board to serve as
board liaisons to standing committees.

Ask current committee chairs
to secure assistant chairs.

■

Secure a home page for your organization
on the World Wide Web.

■

Instruct your staff to always identify
oneself when answering the phone.

■

When warranted, take time to thank
co-workers with a sincere handwritten note.

To enhance the Strategic Planning Committee, invite nonboard members to serve on the committee.

◼

Incorporate the process of reviewing the status of the strategic plan at Executive Committee meetings.

◼

Subscribe to the quarterly publication, *Non Profit Management and Leadership*.

Sincerely and appropriately celebrate the
work anniversaries of your employees.

■

Consider changing locks when
an employee termination occurs.

■

Budget monies for employee tuition
reimbursement (establish an annual limit).

■

Use a color-coded filing system
in your office.

Place an advertisement in your local
newspaper for volunteers,
or check to see if the newspaper has a
free listing/column for volunteers.

■

Secure a booth at a nonprofit fair or
shopping mall to promote your organization
and to recruit potential volunteers.

■

Host a "first timers" social event for new
members of your board. This will help
to make members comfortable.

Remember that it is your responsibility
to make your chief elected leader
a hero during his or her term.

At organization activities, recruit volunteers
to staff registration tables, man booths,
and perform day-of-event functions.
Keep yourself free to both trouble shoot
and be a gracious host.

■

Add "Please Post" to the corner of a
promotional flyer so that it is posted
on a bulletin board.

■

Consider volunteer contracts that feature term,
responsibilities, hours per week, etc.

If your organization offers scholarships, consider outsourcing the program via a scholarship management company.

■

For all functions, include a detailed map, address, and phone number of the location with the invitation.

■

When hiring for a full-time professional position, effectively screen the candidates to 1, 2, or 3 candidates. Then, present these finalists to the board for final review.

To develop teamwork, form an outside-of-the-office staff sporting activity (softball, bowling, golf, etc.).

■

Give a pumpkin to each staff member during Halloween week.

■

Develop a culture change by redefining your volunteers as unsalaried employees.

When building partnerships with for-profit businesses, research, discuss, and market the partnership on a win-win basis (understand the for-profit business's reason for participating).

To secure volunteers from a corporation, give the company payroll-size information sheets to be included with its employees' pay checks.

When receiving a potential gift-in-kind, carefully review the donation in terms of further costs and liabilities. Some gifts may burden your organization.

■

When planning meetings, social events, and other activities, select sites that offer ample, free parking, pay phones, and vending services.

■

When traveling for business, always carry twenty $1 bills.

Build continuous executive leadership from the board. Identify potential future leaders and invite them to executive committee meetings, as an occasional guest.

■

When appropriate and warranted, occasionally offer an employee a Friday afternoon off.

■

Become familiar with the goals and objectives of your regional community foundation (secure their guidelines).

When a relevant or related article
about your organization is in the news,
clip and route the piece to all co-workers
and/or board members.

■

Adapt a working format for board meetings
during the meal section of the gathering.
Seat members at round tables, then ask
that members at each table discuss an
organization topic. To assist the process,
identify a leader at each table.

To recognize a co-worker's
accomplishment, post several colorful,
handmade congratulatory signs
at his or her work station.

■

One weekend before an important
activity, use e-mail or a fax broadcast
to issue a last-minute reminder.

■

Personally make an annual financial
donation to your organization.
This demonstrates your commitment.

Remember that an effective nonprofit
board includes the three Cs and two Gs:
cash, clout, and contacts
and give money or get money.

■

Confirm that each board committee has a
charter (and confirm that it is current).

■

When developing board-related task forces,
consider the advantages of assigning just
one person or a two-person group.

Consider hiring outside, independent
consultants to assist in the
board evaluation process.

■

Remember, an advisory committee
does not have legal authority, does not
govern, and should not make policy.

■

Accept credit card payments, and encourage
your constituents to pay by this method.

Secure as a donation, the services of a
public relations expert to improve your
organization's image and status
in the community.

■

The chief staff officer of your
organization should be a member of the
Strategic Planning Committee.

■

Never make a promise to your board
or staff that you cannot keep.

If an individual voices a legitimate concern or complaint regarding your organization, visit him or her to address the concern face to face.

■

Consider the advantages of a professional fundraising workshop to create the appropriate fund development attitude for board members.

■

Each morning, greet and exchange pleasantries with your co-workers.

Before each activity that uses audio/visual equipment, thoroughly test each machine, learn how it works, and test lighting.

As a family-oriented fundraising
activity, organize a miniature golf outing.
Consider soliciting pledges.

■

Personally, and tactfully, invite nonactive
board members to become involved
in one aspect of the organization.

■

Consult your legal experts when by-laws
or personnel policies are being modified.

Written communications should always include a post script that reiterates pertinent information.

■

Hire a press clipping service to monitor the press your organization receives.

■

Annually, conduct a board/staff luncheon to fully recognize staff achievements.

Become a mentor for a
new nonprofit manager.

Distribute your organization's newsletter
to past, present, and potential stakeholders.
(Update the database twice a year.)

◼

Subscribe to *Association Trends.*

◼

Provide donors with an alternative style
of contribution by equating their contribution
to a specific item their monetary gift will buy.

Consider two-tier board seats for voting
and nonvoting positions.

■

Confirm that all your
donor profiles are current.

■

As a fundraising activity, consider
corporate casual days where businesses
permit their employees to dress down
for a charity fee/donation.

Each December, print and distribute
a one-page, 12-month calendar that
includes your organization's name, logo,
address, and phone and fax numbers.

■

Earn the Certified Association
Executive distinction.

Enhance VIP name badges by adding preprinted, self-adhesive color ribbons that identify the wearer as a board member, exhibitor, volunteer, and so forth.

■

Thoroughly understand and use during meetings *Robert's Rules of Order.*
Obtain a paperback edition of the book.

■

Use actors to portray historical figures to enhance the atmosphere at social events.

Consider organizing a purchasing
group with neighboring nonprofit
organizations or chapters.

When invited, personally attend business celebrations of your members or volunteers (e.g., grand openings, anniversaries, etc.).

◼

On the successful completion of large-scale projects, reward the responsible staff with balloons or flowers delivered to their home.

◼

Remember, when all measures have been exhausted, your final recourse must be to terminate a volunteer.

Employ a professional development consultant for a specific fundraising event or to evaluate the organization's total development efforts. Confirm the consultant's credentials and contact references.

■

To improve attendance and visibility, schedule meetings or events jointly or concurrently with related organizations.

■

Identify the foundations in your geographic area. Then research their funding priorities.

Refine your organization's budget to reflect direct, program-related costs from general administrative expenses.

∎

As a staff or volunteer benefit, affiliate your organization with a nearby community credit union.

∎

Evaluate your member benefits programs continuously. (Are they truly meeting the needs of your constituents?)

Always stay informed of political trends
or actions that may affect your organization
or the nonprofit industry.

Be able to readily distinguish
your organization's attributes from
those with similar purposes.

Offer unemployed members a
reduced membership fee.

In your organization's newsletter and annual report, always print all volunteers' names in boldface.

Develop positive working relationships
with representatives of the major
periodicals of your region.

∎

Publish photographs of your board members
in your board manual.

∎

On all internal handwritten notes to staff,
always close the message with "thanks."

Encourage each staff member to maintain
an updated list of co-workers' home phone
numbers, for emergenies.

∎

Develop for new employees, a one-page
questionnaire for staff orientation purposes.
This could be used as an ice breaker.

∎

Conduct a brief, but thorough,
exit interview with resigning staff.

Publish a book detailing the history
of your organization/chapter.

∎

Buy customized Christmas/holiday
ornaments featuring your organization's logo
to award to volunteers and staff or to sell.

∎

When approaching a special anniversary
year for your organization, highlight the
accomplishment by printing an anniversary
message on your organization's envelopes,
stationery, and newsletter.

Print testimonials from your satisfied
volunteers and/or members
in your organization's newsletter.

■

Subscribe to and read the
Wall Street Journal.

■

Purchase additional copies of this book
for co-workers as birthday gifts
or holiday presents.

Resources

American Society of Association Executives, 1575 Eye St., NW, Washington, DC 20005 (202/626-ASAE).

Association Trends, 7910 Woodmont Ave., Bethesda, MD 20814 (301/652-8666).

CEO Update and CEO Job Opportunities Update, 1575 Eye St., NW, Ste 1190, Washington, DC 20005 (202/408-7900).

Certified Association Executive, American Society of Association Executives, 1575 Eye St., NW, Washington, DC 20005 (202/626-ASAE).

Community Accountants (refer to your local white pages).

Continuing Education Units. Contact: International Association for Continuing Education and Training, 1200 19th St., NW, Ste 300, Washington, DC 20036 (202/857-1122).

The Chronicle of Philanthropy, 1255 Twenty-third St., NW, Washington, DC 20037 (202/466-1200); or P.O. Box 1989, Marion, OH 43309-2089.

Dale Carnegie & Associates, 1465 Franklin Ave., Garden City, NY 11530 (516/248-5100).

The Foundation Directory, c/o The Foundation Center, 79 Fifth Ave., New York, NY 10003-3076 (212/620-4230).

Institutes for Organization Management, Center for Leadership Development, 1615 H St., NW, Washington, DC 20062-2000 (202/463-5570).

Leadership Classes, National Association for Community Leadership, 200 South Merdian St., Ste 340, Indianapolis, IN 46225 (317/637-7408).

The Mandel Center for Non-Profit Organizations, Case Western Reserve University, 10900 Euclid Ave., Cleveland, OH 44106 (216/368-4623).

Myers-Briggs Type Indicator Test, c/o Consulting Psychologists Press, 3808 East Bayshore Rd., Palo Alto, CA 94303 (415/969-8901).

National Center for Non-Profit Boards, 2000 L St., NW, Ste 510, Washington, DC 20036-4907 (202/452-6262).

National Executive Service Corporation, 257 Park Ave. South, 2d Fl., New York, NY 10010 (212/529-6660).

National Society of Fund-Raising Executives, 1101 King St., Ste 700, Alexandria, VA 22314-2967 (703/684-0410).

Non-Profit Management and Leadership, c/o Jossey-Bass Publishers, 350 Sansome St., San Francisco, CA 94104.

Non-Profit Survival Network, 150 Third St., Box 226, Akron, IA 51001 (712/568-2418).

The Non-Profit Times, 240 Cedar Knolls Rd., Ste 318, Cedar Knolls, NJ 07928 (201/734-1700).

Toastmasters International, P.O. Box 9052, Mission Viejo, CA 92690 (714/858-8255).

About the Author

Richard J. Maladecki has been employed in the nonprofit sector since 1975. He has worked for both 501(c)(3) and 501(c)(6) organizations during his nonprofit career. Currently, he is the executive director of the Electrical Association of Philadelphia.

In 1995, Mr. Maladecki received a master's of science degree in Nonprofit Management from Eastern College of St. Davids, Pa. Mr. Maladecki volunteers for several regional and national organizations that share the common mission of nonprofit industry advancement. He has presented many seminars and workshops on various aspects and disciplines relating to nonprofit management. Mr. Maladecki and his family reside in Berwyn, Pa.

A Moment, Please

We'd like to hear from you. If you have an idea or advice to share with your colleagues in nonprofit organizations, please complete this form and send it in.

Your Name _____

Organization _____

City/State/Zip _____

Phone (_____) _____

Idea _____

_____

_____

Mail to:
Bits, Tips & Power Points • P.O. Box 987 • Valley Forge, PA 19482-0987
Fax to: (610) 917-9562